MW01101990

CLOTHING
in Art

Words that appear in **bold** type are defined in the glossary on pages 28 and 29.

Please visit our web site at: **www.garethstevens.com**
For a free color catalog describing Gareth Stevens Publishing's
list of high-quality books and multimedia programs, call
1-800-542-2595 (USA) or 1-800-387-3178 (Canada).
Gareth Stevens Publishing's fax: (414) 332-3567.

Library of Congress Cataloging-in-Publication Data

Baumbusch, Brigitte.
    Clothing in art / by Brigitte Baumbusch.
        p. cm. — (What makes a masterpiece?)
    Includes index.
    ISBN 0-8368-4780-6 (lib. bdg.)
    1. Clothing and dress in art—Juvenile literature. I. Title.
    N8217.C63B38   2005
    704.9'49391—dc22   2005041471

This edition first published in 2006 by
Gareth Stevens Publishing
A Member of the WRC Media Family of Companies
330 West Olive Street, Suite 100
Milwaukee, Wisconsin 53212 USA

Copyright © Andrea Dué s.r.l. 2003

This U.S. edition copyright © 2006 by Gareth Stevens, Inc.
Additional end matter copyright © 2006 by Gareth Stevens, Inc.

Translator: Erika Pauli

Gareth Stevens series editor: Dorothy L. Gibbs
Gareth Stevens art direction: Tammy West

Printed in the United States of America

1 2 3 4 5 6 7 8 9 09 08 07 06 05

CLOTHING in Art

by Brigitte Baumbusch

GARETH**STEVENS**
GS
PUBLISHING
A Member of the WRC Media Family of Companies

What makes clothing . . .

In the late 1700s, Francisco Goya painted this **portrait** of a Spanish lady wearing a white dress. The lady's dog is white, like the dress, and has a red ribbon on one leg to match the red bows of its mistress.

In stark **contrast** to Goya's Spanish lady are two young women (below) wearing very dark clothing. They were painted a century later by Renoir, a French **Impressionist**.

a masterpiece?

Some clothing has checks.

This figure clothed in an unusual checkered **garment** appeared in a **medieval** book made in Ireland more than 1,300 years ago.

In 1908, French **naive** painter Henri Rousseau **portrayed** this little girl in a red-and-white polka-dot dress, sitting in a field dotted with red and white flowers.

Some clothing has dots.

Clothing can be splendid . . .

The man in this magnificent outfit **adorned** with pearls and precious gemstones is Henry VIII, a great English king of the sixteenth century. This portrait was painted by the younger of two German artists named Hans Holbein. They were father and son.

or simple.

The generously sized clothing on this Chinese man is as simple and comfortable as a **dressing gown**. It was drawn by a Japanese artist about seven hundred years ago.

Clothes are the fashions of long ago . . .

This **figurine** was made in Iran four thousand years ago.
The rather **robust** woman is wearing a dress made of
carefully arranged strips of wool.

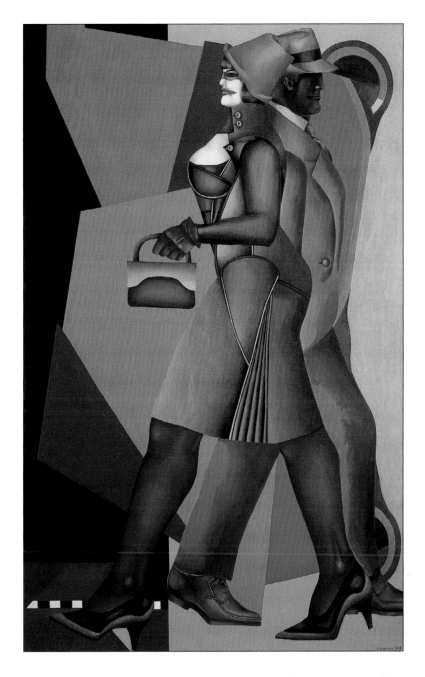

German-born American artist Richard Lindner is known for his **quirky "pop" art**. This painting portrays two passersby of the 1960s.

and of today.

Clothes can be ordinary . . .

"Serious" English clothing — shirt, tie, suit jacket, and bowler hat — poses next to its undressed owner in this painting by Belgian **surrealist** René Magritte.

This **porcelain statuette**, made in Germany in the middle of the eighteenth century, **depicts** the gaily colored costume of Harlequin, a central character in Italian comic theater.

extraordinary . . .

14

comfortable . . .

The woman to the left is Athena, an **ancient** Greek goddess. Although comfortably dressed in a loose-fitting garment with a **peplum**, she is also wearing a helmet. Athena is a warrior goddess.

Wearing a comfortable pair of overalls and a wide-brimmed straw hat, the little boy in this 1927 portrait (below) by Mexican artist Diego Rivera is ready to play in the sun.

or cumbersome.

In centuries past, children were often dressed to look just like adults. In a full-skirted gown with a tightly fitted **bodice**, the little girl to the left looks like a miniature lady. Her portrait was painted in Russia in the 1700s.

Voluminous garments surround this seventeenth-century Japanese woman (below). Seated on the ground, she almost looks like a bird with an enormous, fanlike tail.

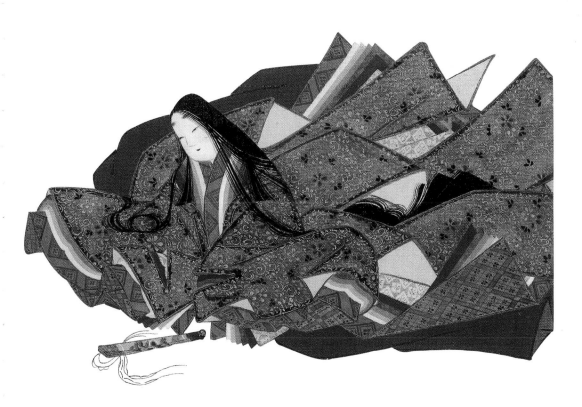

Clothes tell tales...

A procession of women dressed in long, decorative robes was painted in the early twentieth century as an illustration for *The Thousand and One Nights*, a collection of old Arabian fairy tales.

dance . . .

The dress on this ballerina makes her look like a flower. It was painted in the nineteenth century by French Impressionist Edgar Degas, who was fascinated with ballet and the theater.

This **ornate** costume was used in **Tibet** for a dance known as the "Dance of the Black Hat." The **satin** garment is at least one hundred years old.

INVS PHLIPPVS HISPANVS DESCOLARIS   RELATOR VICTORIE THEVC

and fight battles.

Long ago, warriors and soldiers dressed in iron, called armor, to protect themselves.

A **fresco** (far left) by Andrea del Castagno, an Italian **Renaissance** painter, depicts a fierce army leader wearing armor and carrying a sword.

The armor of a Japanese warrior of the past (right) was made of iron and leather.

A helmet to protect the head was often part of a soldier's armor. This **gilded bronze** helmet (bottom left) is shaped like an animal's head, perhaps to frighten the soldier's enemies.

A walking stick, at one time . . .

Walking sticks like the ones below, with porcelain handles in different shapes and designs, were made in Naples, Italy, more than two hundred years ago.

This **Parisian** gentleman is fashionably dressed in late nineteenth-century style. He was painted by Giovanni Boldini, an Italian artist who settled in Paris in 1871.

was a sign of a well-dressed man . . .

and all
well-dressed ladies . . .

A lady painted in 1914 by German artist August
Macke stopped to admire hats in a shop window.

In the early 1900s, American artist Mary Cassatt painted this portrait (above) of a little girl wearing a big bonnet.

wore hats.

This figure of a woman (bottom left) wearing an elaborate **headdress** comes from Indonesia. It is made of braided palm leaves.

GLOSSARY

adorned
decorated with beautiful ornaments
or objects

ancient
relating to a period in history from the
earliest civilizations until about the time
of the Roman Empire

bodice
the portion of a woman's dress that
extends from the shoulders to the waist

bronze
a hard metal alloy (combination of two or
more metals) that is a mixture of mainly
copper and tin

contrast
(n) a comparison of two somewhat similar
objects to determine their differences

depicts
shows or describes by means of a picture

dressing gown
a robe that is worn while getting dressed,
resting, or relaxing

figurine
a small, decorative, statuelike object, usually
made of china, pottery, wood, or metal

fresco
a painting on a wall, especially a painting
done on fresh, damp plaster, using water-
based paints or coloring

garment
a main article or item of clothing, distinct
from shoes, hats, or other wearable items
that are considered accessories

gilded
covered with a thin layer of a metallic
gold or silver coating

headdress
an usually large and elaborate covering
for the head

Impressionist
one of the French painters of the 1870s
who used strokes and dabs of primary
colors to create the appearance or
impression of natural, reflected light

medieval
belonging to the Middle Ages, a period
of history in Europe from the end of the
Roman Empire to the 1500s

naive
self-taught, rather than formally schooled
in the rules and technical aspects of art

ornate
highly decorative, often having elaborate, intricate, or flowery designs

Parisian
from or having to do with the city of Paris, in France

peplum
a short strip of gathered fabric attached at the waistline of a dress, blouse, or jacket

"pop" art
a style of modern art in which common, everyday objects, such as hamburgers and soup cans, are the subjects of paintings and sculptures and may even be used as materials for works of art

porcelain
a delicate, white, ceramic material used to make fine china dishes and figurines

portrait
a painting or photograph of a person, often showing just the head, neck, and shoulders

portrayed
pictured, especially in the style of a portrait

quirky
having unusual or unnatural characteristics

Renaissance
a period of European history, between the Middle Ages (14th century) and modern times (17th century), during which learning flourished and interest in classical (relating to ancient Greek and Roman civilizations) art and literature was renewed, or "reborn"

robust
having a sturdy, strong, or hearty appearance

satin
a tightly woven, silky fabric that is shiny on the surface but dull on the back

statuette
a statue that is usually small enough and lightweight enough to be held in the hands

surrealist
an artist or writer whose work is more dreamlike than realistic

Tibet
a cold, wasteland region of China, isolated by some of the world's highest mountains and where even the valleys are at higher elevations than most mountains of the world

voluminous
long and full with a lot of volume or bulk and often having many folds or gathers

PICTURE LIST

page 4 – Francisco Goya (1746-1828): The White Duchess, 1795. Portrait of the duchess of Alba (Spain). Private property. Photo Scala Archives.

page 5 – Pierre-Auguste Renoir (1841-1919): Two Young Women. Moscow, Pushkin Museum. Photo Scala Archives.

page 6 – Man, symbol of St. Matthew, miniature from the "Book of Durrow." Medieval Irish art of the late 7th century. Dublin, Trinity College Library. Drawing by Sauro Giampaia.

page 7 – Henri Rousseau (1844-1910): Child with Doll, 1908. Paris, Musée de l'Orangerie. Photo Scala Archives.

page 8 – Hans Holbein the Younger (1497-1543): Portrait of Henry VIII. Rome, National Gallery. Photo Scala Archives.

page 9 – Muromachi Kao (13th to 14th centuries): Kanzan. Washington, Freer Gallery of Art. Drawing by Sauro Giampaia.

page 10 – Figurine of a woman, in steatite (soapstone) and limestone. Elamite art, early 2nd millennium B.C., from Bactria (Iran). Paris, Louvre. Drawing by Sauro Giampaia.

page 11 – Richard Lindner (1901-1978): The Moon of Alabama, 1963.

Private property. Photo Scala Archives. © Richard Lindner by SIAE, 2003.

page 12 – René Magritte (1898-1967): The Way to Damascus. Private property. Photo Artothek. © René Magritte by SIAE, 2003.

page 13 – Statuette of a seated Harlequin. Meissen porcelain, mid-18th century. Milan, Museo Teatrale alla Scala. Photo Scala Archives.

page 14 – Marble relief of a musing Athena. Greek art, 5th century B.C. Athens, Acropolis Museum. Drawing by Sauro Giampaia.

page 15 – Diego Rivera (1886-1957): Ignacio Sanchez, 1927. Private property. Photo Artothek. © Diego Rivera by Fideocomiso Diego Rivera, 2003.

page 16 – Ivan Vishniakov (18th century): Portrait of Sara Eleonora Fermor. Saint Petersburg, Russian State Museum. Photo Scala Archives.

page 17 – Tosa school (18th century): The poetess Onono-Komaki. Genoa, Edoardo Chiossone Museum of Oriental Art. Photo Scala Archives.

pages 18-19 – Vittorio Zecchin (1878-1947): panel for "The Thousand

and One Nights." Private property. Photo Scala Archives.

page 20 – Edgar Degas (1834-1917): The Star, or Dancer on Stage. Paris, Musée d'Orsay. Photo Peter Willi / Artothek.

page 21 – Costume in Chinese satin, damask, and brocade for the Dance of the Black Hat. Tibetan art of the 19th to 20th centuries. Newark, Newark Museum. Photo Art Resource / Scala.

page 22 – Andrea del Castagno (1419-1457): Pippo Spano. Florence, Uffizi. Photo Scala Archives.

Parade helmet in gilded bronze. Italian art of the 16th century. Paris, Louvre. Photo Scala Archives.

page 23 – Iron and leather armor. Japanese art of the 16th century. Genoa, Edoardo Chiossone Museum of Oriental Art. Photo Scala Archives.

page 24 – Three walking sticks with porcelain handles. Capodimonte porcelain, 18th century. Naples, Museo Nazionale Duca di Martina. Photo Scala Archives.

page 25 – Giovanni Boldini (1842-1931): Portrait of Count Robert de Montesquieu, 1897. Paris, Musée d'Orsay. Photo Scala Archives.

page 26 – August Macke (1887-1914): Lady with a Parasol in Front of the Window of a Hat Shop, 1914. Essen, Folkwang Museum. Photo Artothek.

Detail of a sacrificial offering in braided palm leaves ("Cili"), depicting the divinity (god or goddess) for whom it was made. Indonesian art of the early 20th century. Munich, State Museum of Ethnography. Drawing by Sauro Giampaia.

page 27 – Mary Cassatt (1845-1926): Sara in a Green Bonnet, c. 1901. Washington, Smithsonian American Art Museum. Photo Art Resource / Scala.

INDEX